Effective

Blog Commenting

By
Kef Hollenbach

Purpose, Acknowledgement & Second Edition

PURPOSE:

This report is written to provide information about Internet Blog Commenting.

Every effort has been made to make this report as complete and accurate as possible. However, there may be mistakes in typography or content. This report provides information on Blog Commenting only up to the publishing date. Therefore, this report should be used as a guide - not as the ultimate source of Internet Blog Commenting.

The purpose of this report is to educate. The author and the publisher do not warrant the information contained is fully complete and shall not be responsible for any errors or omissions. The author and publisher shall have neither liability nor responsibility to any person or entity with respect to any loss or damage caused or alleged to be caused directly or indirectly by this report.

ACKNOWLEDGEMENT:

Thanks to Peter Edunet, Web Master for internet marketing KY, LLC, for pointing out some of the examples used. Additionally, I wish to thank Mr. Edunet for reviewing this report. No compensation was made to Mr. Edunet.

SECOND EDITION:

The first edition included hyperlinks to the posts and comments discussed. The concept was to make the report as short as possible by not including all the comment's complete text.

The author, publisher, and proofreader all missed the very important fact that several Kindle models do not have a browser so have extreme difficulty with clicking a hyperlink to see what was being discussed or used as an example.

In this edition, the hyperlinks have been replaced by the comments cited. A reference list at the end is in the same sequence as the comments and contain the commenter's name, date and time; along with the URL of the post on which the comment is made.

The comments cited as examples contain the writer's original grammar, spelling and syntax.

This second edition is completely self-contained for older versions of the Kindle.

COPYRIGHT:

Text copyright © 2012 by internet marketing KY, LLC

All rights reserved. No part of this publication may be reproduced or transmitted in any form or by any means, electronic, or mechanical, including photocopying, recording, or by any information storage and retrieval system.

All comments cited are the property of their respective owners and are used here with the permission of Mr. Peter Edunet, Web Master.

All clip art is the property of Microsoft Corp. and is used under the Microsoft End-User-License-Agreement (EULA) found at http://download.microsoft.com/documents/useterms/Word_2003_English_4afa6519-df62-4421-b90a-5b756d7cf0ac.pdf

internet marketing KY, LLC
Louisville, KY 40204
E-Mail: internetmarketingKY@gmail.com

Table of Contents

Introduction

Beware of drive-by comments

"Keep It Real"

Reading the post

Timing your comments

Winning Techniques for Blog Commenting

HOW To Differentiate Your Comments

Conclusion

Introduction

A blogger has asked you for "professional blog commenting," You open a post on the specified blog and make a random comment, "hey, nice post. It really helped!" Does this fulfill the desired goals? No! There are several important points to keep in mind if you want to make your blog comments, effective and valuable to readers!

Do you know that the quality of blog comments on a blog post reflects its popularity, authority and success?

Blog comments show whether the blog has a quality readership and how engaged the audience is. This works like a positive feedback cycle, if a blog has a loyal following, it will attract more readers and the audience will keep on multiplying. On the contrary, if the blog is full of ineffective posts and spammy comments, chances of it getting a quality response ever, are slim!

If you are a professional blog commenter, this guide will help you understand the essential factors that make your blog comment valuable, to the blog owner as well as the blog readers, with live examples. These examples demonstrate the techniques you use to make your comments fruitful and valuable to readers!

"Take Time for All Things – Great Haste Makes Great Waste" – Franklin, Benjamin

Beware of drive-by comments

As a blog commenter, you must be aware of the comments that come in the category of "drive-by" comments - the name itself gives away the meaning of the term.

These are the comments that are spammy and do not add value or give any benefit to a blog. Consider the one mentioned in the first line of this report:

"Hey, nice post. It really helped!"

OR

"Wow! I didn't know that! Thanks for sharing!! Check this post: www.xyz.com/xyz"

Characteristics of a drive-by comment
- Doesn't take time to write.
- Doesn't contain a solid opinion on at least one aspect of the blog post.
- Does not reflect in any way that the blog post was read.

Avoid making drive-by comments
Do you want to read more or depend on what information is given in a blog that has a lot of such comments? Such blogs have a spammy audience whose sole purpose is to advertise their own links and products and have no desire or intention to return to the blog! Credible bloggers would rather not let spammy, useless comments pass through their comments' spam filters.

Drive-by comments show you haven't read the post and have just made the comment for the sake of making it – or, even if you have read the post, you have not given much thought to what it says! Your comment does not highlight at least one aspect of the post in a realistic way.

A generic comment such as **"I never knew about these facts! Wow !"** does not even indicate the post may have been read.

"Keep It Real"

Give a quick glance to the comment made by Ann relating to ashes from wood burning stoves:

> Ann on January 2, 2012 at 7:44 pm said:
>
> i can't believe i didn't know this information, some of it my dad was just explaining to me because he and my mom just got a wood burning stove. he is using wood from his acreage anytime a tree falls or needs to be trimmed. but it really is important to know what kind of wood you are using and what to expect from it. he was burning some pine and it smelled great, but made scary popping noises because of the sap.

The blog post tells the readers about what type of logs are effective for better heating, when used in a wood burning stove. Observe the way the commenter has related to the post, naturally. Supposing this commenter is not telling a real-life story, can you guess it isn't true? No. See how the commenter has related the blog post to his/her situation making the comment sound realistic. It is not nonsense either, although the comment may be "made-up", the content adds value to the blog post, giving an example of a situation another reader can relate to and learn from.

Reading the post

How does one come up with a "natural" blog comment? When you read a news headline, for example, you do get a spontaneous, original opinion of the news piece that gets more refined and complete as you read the complete news article, right? Now when you talk to your friends about it, you discuss it with your own perspective. Treat blog posts in exactly the same way.

"Quality is never an accident. It  is always the result of intelligent effort"
– John Ruskin

Making tailored comments look natural can be tricky! Professional comments **reflect that the commenter first read the post, gave some real thought on the subject matter and then formed a proper opinion about the information it provides.** They also maintain a balance by covering only one or two aspects of a post instead of unnecessarily commenting on each and every point. See how Jimmy demonstrates this in:

> jimmy on June 25, 2012 at 12:06 am said:
>
> I am glad to know that the canvas covers are not only the cheaper option but are better for warmer climates. We just moved across the country so we are not used to the warmer climate and had no idea what to look for in a cover for the futon we had from college. Moving across country took alot of money so we are on a budget so this is good news.

Make your blog comments more sustainable, more natural, - and more valuable to readers.

Reading posts and commenting is one way to begin developing a sense of the issues, the pros & cons, the topics within a subject.

Timing your comments

For most other jobs such as, designing a website for a client, a short delivery time is a good thing. For effective blog commenting, it isn't - particularly when you are asked to comment on a single blog with 10 posts. Would 2-day or 4-day delivery be natural in this case? No. Change that to 10-days (1 or 2 comments a day, 5-days a week for 2 calendar weeks) and you are on the right track. Also, for a case like this, ask the blog owner or webmaster just what they expect you to accomplish!

Winning Techniques for Blog Commenting

In addition to loving your work and being enthusiastic about it, you can use any of the following comment techniques to make your blog comments effective.

1) **Making Statements**

    Your comment can be a simple statement, as long as it is well thought-out and reflects that you understood the post.

    See what Kim Moore says about the post, "Canadian Government Undertakes Major Challenge To Make Wood Burning Stoves Greener" A simple two liner but an ideal example of quality:

    > Kim Moore on October 20, 2011 at 1:41 pm said:
    >
    > Just when you thought that wood burning stoves won't get any better! Hopefully, this will encourage more people to use them! Thank you, Canadian government!

    Jeana, on this post about nail biting remedies, also writes a two-liner comment containing a powerful statement:

jeana @ 2012-7-5 20:38

> Those situations yes were extreme but it put a good image in your mind. Sometimes you need to be jolted in order to become motivated to change.

2) **Praising**

Praising is good because it shows the blog post is helpful. Be careful with this though, it is easy to go overboard when praising and this is a spammer tactic! There's hardly a chance of a blog post containing life changing information. Even if it does, there will be ample proof of this; the number of commenters and the quality of their comments will authenticate the value of the post. However if there is a solitary glowing comment on a post it is likely to be considered as fake and spammy.

Look at the comment by Arsepa on a post about playing games online safely:

> Arsepa on May 21, 2012 at 9:36 pm said:
>
> I have to express appaecirtion to the writer just for rescuing me from this trouble. As a result of browsing throughout the search engines and getting concepts which are not beneficial, I thought my entire life was done. Existing without the approaches to the difficulties you have fixed by way of the site is a crucial case, and the kind that might have in a wrong way affected my entire career if I hadn't encountered your blog post. Your own

mastery and kindness in handling all the stuff was useful. I am not sure what I would've done if I hadn't come upon such a step like this. I can at this time look ahead to my future. Thanks so much for the skilled and sensible guide. I will not be reluctant to suggest your blog post to anyone who will need assistance on this topic.

Now compare it with Lynette's comment on a post about insomnia:

lynette on August 8, 2012 at 9:19 pm said:

I think this is a great list, I agree with all of them. I have started sleeping with a fan for the white noise and have noticed that it is a lot easier to sleep. Not only fall asleep but stay asleep and that has been a big issue in the past. I do notice that if my routine is off at all I have a harder time sleeping.

See the difference? People can view Arsepa's praising as excessive (though it may not necessarily be so in this case), if they find the content of the post does not deserve this level of praise. As an effective blog commenter, going with Lynette's approach while praising, is much more believable. Her comment mildly indicates what she found helpful and how.

3) **Disagreeing**
There are things you may not agree with. Sometimes a casual reader expresses disagreement. So does an

effective blog commenter - only where necessary. Being respectful and stating what you disagree with in the style of expressing an opinion, is the way to go.

A generic example is "I don't think this happens to everyone." Megan's comment on this post about chronic insomnia is a better, live example that demonstrates the "disagreeing tactic":

> megan on July 29, 2012 at 10:28 pm said:
>
> I have to disagree on a few of the potential causes of sleep deprivation. I know several people myself included that need some kind of noise to sleep. I use a fan at night, I find it actually helps lull me to sleep. Secondly, if you need sleep and are not getting it at night wouldn't a nap if your able during the day actually be beneficial?

Megan disagrees on some of the points in the post with a logical argument, and the blog writer John C., answers her comment to clarify the facts. Notice how this can be helpful to all the future readers of this blog?

> John C on July 31, 2012 at 5:47 pm said:
>
> Hi Megan,
> Fan noise is a good 'white noise'; which has been shown to help some insomnia sufferers. Several decades ago one of the most popular 'white noises' was sea sounds/surf sounds. 'White noise' may even have an underlying rhythm which in turn assists with falling asleep (isochiral

music and brain entrainment are more technical terms.)

Most sleep professionals believe a nap tends to rejuvenate a person. While naps are being found beneficial since they do refresh the napper, they also may postpone when that person begins feeling drowsy.

Highlighting anything that is vague is a "disagreeing comment." It gives another commenter or the blog writer the chance to answer with information that adds value to the original blog post.

4) **Answering another Comment**

A previous commenter may have asked a question, if you know the answer, this can be an easy way to make a natural comment that truly adds value for the next reader. See how Jon Jadesston answers Kayla's question about availability of essential oils in the stores, in this post about natural remedies for insomnia:

> Jon Jadesston on June 17, 2012 at 2:25 pm said:
>
> A lot of every-day pharmacies carry those oils. Might be slightly pricey or may not be the highest quality. I usually think some careful research between a holistic food store and online will provide the highest quality.
>
> Surprisingly, fewer drops means a tremendous increase in value.

5) **Initiating Dialogue with another Commenter**
   Striking up a conversation with another commenter can be a great way to add value to a post! You can disagree, elaborate on a vague point in the post, ask questions about his or her experience regarding a topic and what not.

   John C., the blog writer, conversationally responds to Cindy's comment on this post about non-medication treatments for insomnia:

   > John C on June 11, 2012 at 3:28 pm said:
   >
   > Hi Cindy,
   > That alone is a great first step! You might also think about using an entrainment method; usually effective for 50-75% of chronic insomniacs. The "effective" range can vary, but a very low cost and <u>non-supplement way to approach insomnia</u>.

   He even adds a relevant cross-link to another post of the blog in this comment, demonstrating how an effective commenter can follow a similar tactic as an effective way to enhance the inter-connectedness of information presented.

6) **Initiating Dialogue with Blog Writer/Web Master**
   Asking questions about something mentioned in a blog post from the writer, is probably one of the simplest

approaches to make a relevant comment. Don't ask irrelevant and unnecessary questions though.

When you ask a question about something ambiguous in the original post, you open up the possibility for the blog writer or another commenter to add valuable related content to the post, as an "answer comment." This increases the overall value of the post, for future readers.

See how Kevin A. answers some good questions related to his posts on Natural Remedies Hypothyroidism by Tanya:

> tanya on May 22, 2012 at 9:48 pm said:
>
> Well sounds like several of those natural remedies are things that you likely use daily in your cooking or at least often like cayenne pepper. If I use those in my diet will this help prevent hyperthyroidism? Are all of them stuff you can find in food? If so it sounds like a quick trip to the health store would do me some good.
>
> Kevin A. on May 23, 2012 at 6:36 am said:
>
> Hello Tanya,
> Many chronic conditions are effected by the food we eat. Please keep in mind that each person's digestion efficiency and lifestyle also impact a predilection towards or away from a chronic condition. Sensitivity and allergic

reactions also dictate what we should, can and should not consume.

Most, but not all the time, a natural remedy for hypothyroidism is safe. How long it takes to be effective is impacted by many variables. How effective it may be depends on your particular digestion efficiency, other conditions, sensitivities and lifestyle. If you are able to see a naturopathic or homeopathic trained health care practitioner, we encourage you to get that personalized direction.

and Preety:

Preety on May 9, 2012 at 6:53 am said:

what is monk pepper known in india?

Kevin A. on May 10, 2012 at 6:52 pm said:

Hi,
Monk's Pepper is also known as:
chaste tree berry
safe tree
Indian-spice
wild pepper
vitex
agnus-castus
chasteberry
Abraham's Balm
cloister pepper

Some Hindi and other Indian terms are:
Sambhalu
Nirgundi

The genus/species in Latin is:
Vitex negundo

HOW to Differentiate Your Comments

The "answer another comment" (#4) could include **a deep-link to another post on the blog.** Most of the time this is not possible, but really nice when it is done! See how Vickie R. uses this approach to answer Jimmy's comment on "How to Pick A Memory Foam Mattress":

Vickie R on August 16, 2012 at 7:48 am said:

@Missy M, Great post indeed. I'm an avid follower of your blog – being a natural memory foam proponent; I love to see other people creating awareness about it.

@jimmy, i'm compelled to comment on your question. Anyone who does have such a mattress should surely get a replacement for it, and get a natural memory foam instead. You can't reduce the chemicals when a mattress is actually made up of them, you can perhaps hide the smell but can't take away the chemicals, they will stay right there in any case, won't they? There's a great post I read on this blog that answers your question (in case you missed it) "How to get a memory foam cheap" reading it you'll know that although the replacement looks like a pricey option, it actually isn't .

Another example of a commenter linking to another post on the blog is Tayler's comment on "What Are the Health Issues for the Adult Nail Biter":

> tayler @ 2011-6-25 22:59
>
> It's true there are tons of health problems related to biting nails your hands touch tons of stuff and when put in your mouth you open yourself up to tons of germs and thus diseases. Plus the nails can scratch your gums and get infected. http://www.stopnailbiting.net/nail-biting-effects.html lists other health potential problems.

Taylor's comment is not an answer to another commenter's question yet is beneficial for the readers of this particular blog post while **simultaneously giving SEO benefit to the blog**.

'Relevant' and 'well-placed' are blog commenting mantras! That raises an interesting point: the number of posts on a blog directly influences the number of comments and the number of cross-links you can make.

- An **outbound link to an Authority Site** contained in your blog comment illustrates some real thought on a subject. Your comment could contain an outbound link to Wikipedia.org, WebMD.com, even to an Amazon Review page for a product.

    You can apply this technique with almost any of the six styles of comments mentioned above, but it is particularly effective with the "disagreeing" (#3) approach if applicable!

    Look at the comments by tomsbabyjenna and Allena on "Nail Biting, Some Solutions":

    > tomsbabyjenna @ 2011-4-12 23:04
    >
    > I am by nature a picker, for me it's scabs and pimples but I completely understand the uncontrollable urge to pick. I feel like it's a type of self-soothing, you do it to make you feel better. You don't realize all the damage it does. http://www.brainphysics.com/nail-

biting.php talks about other ways to help you get over your need to pick. Some of the ways medicine and psycotherapy. Simply having an accountability partner to bring awareness can help immensly. Since you may not realize your picking someone telling you means your aware and you can do something else.

Allena @ 2011-4-14 16:53

I actually didn't know they had an official name for nail biting, I guess you learn something new everyday! So thanks for that, I'll have to find some way to integrate that into a conversation so I sound smarter lol. I know a lot of people who bite their nails, its super common, I think they figure since everyone else is doing it why bother to stop, its also not hurting anything is an excuse I've heard. This article from the Mayo Clinic http://www.mayoclinic.com/health/nail-biting/AN01144 says theres not any long term damage from biting your nails but does mention the transfer of germs from your hands to your mouth which can cause colds. That alone would make me want to stop. Yuck your hands touch so much stuff and there are so many germs. You can't possibly wash your hands enough to justify getting those germs anywhere near your mouth. Sickenss galore I'm sure!

Both are excellent examples of professional comments that contain outbound links in a way that enhances and adds value to the content of the blog post but does NOT steal the blog's readership.

- **Always go to the blog by way of a Search Engine Response Page (SERP) -** NOT by clicking on a Favorite or copy/pasting the URL from a spreadsheet!

    This is a way to illustrate your grasp of SEO and may have a minor benefit on helping the blog actually rank higher over a period of time.

    Search engines track clicking through to a SERPs site. This is not a big factor but a valuable addition, which makes your blog comments different from all the rest. The down-side is you need to know approximately where a site appears for what keyword phrase.

Conclusion

Surprise! When you follow these 'best practices" you are improving the conversation between readers, site administration and other writers. You have added value for the casual visitor - by clarifying ambiguities, by pointing out logic flaws, or perhaps by beginning or enhancing discussions.

You have also helped the blog gain credibility - both from the readers' as well as the search engines' point of view! How? Witnessing that the blog's audience is involved in improving its content stimulates the interest of new visitors. And, an increasing number of comments on a blog tell search engines that it is getting some engaged, relevant traffic! You have done well.

Feeling good? You deserve to!

Reference
1. Ann on January 2, 2012 at 7:44 pm said:
http://woodburningstovesreviews.net/long-burning-woods-to-use-in-wood-burning-stoves/

2. jimmy on June 25, 2012 at 12:06 am said:
http://cheapfutoncovers.net/futon-covers-all-that-you-need-to-know-338/

3. Kim Moore on October 20, 2011 at 1:41 pm said:
http://woodburningstovesreviews.net/canadian-government-undertakes-major-challenge-to-make-wood-burning-stoves-greener/

4. Arsepa on May 21, 2012 at 9:36 pm said:
http://genghisgamer.com/game-safety-protect-your-online-gamer-accounts-from-being-compromised/

5. megan on July 29, 2012 at 10:28 pm said:
http://remediesforchronicinsomnia.com/chronic-sleep-deprivation-ffects-your-immune-system/

6. The reply to megan by John C on July 31, 2012 at 5:47 pm said:
http://remediesforchronicinsomnia.com/chronic-sleep-deprivation-ffects-your-immune-system/

7. Jon Jadesston on June 17, 2012 at 2:25 pm said:
http://remediesforchronicinsomnia.com/get-a-good-nights-sleep-with-natural-remedies-for-chronic-insomnia/

8. John C on June 11, 2012 at 3:28 pm said:
http://remediesforchronicinsomnia.com/chronic-insomnia-treatments/

9. Tanya on May 22, 2012 at 9:48 pm said:
http://naturalremedieshypothyroidism.com/dr-natasha-paul-about-natural-remedies-for-hypothyroidism/

10. The reply to Tanya by Kevin A. on May 23, 2012 at 6:36 am said:
http://naturalremedieshypothyroidism.com/dr-natasha-paul-about-natural-remedies-for-hypothyroidism/

11. Preety on May 9, 2012 at 6:53 am said:

http://naturalremedieshypothyroidism.com/is-monks-pepper-a-natural-remedy-for-hypothyroidism/

12. The reply to Preety by Kevin A. on May 10, 2012 at 6:52 pm said:
http://naturalremedieshypothyroidism.com/is-monks-pepper-a-natural-remedy-for-hypothyroidism/

13. Vickie R on August 16, 2012 at 7:48 am said:
http://memoryfoammattresscheap.net/how-to-pick-a-memory-foam-mattress/

14. tayler @ 2011-6-25 22:59
http://stopchewingnails.com/what-are-the-health-issues-for-the-adult-nail-biter/

15. tomsbabyjenna @ 2011-4-12 23:04
http://stopchewingnails.com/nail-biting-some-solutions/

16. Allena @ 2011-4-14 16:53
http://stopchewingnails.com/nail-biting-some-solutions/

###

www.ingramcontent.com/pod-product-compliance
Lightning Source LLC
Chambersburg PA
CBHW061523180526
45171CB00001B/309